LOCAL ECUMENISM

HOW CHURCH UNITY IS SEEN AND PRACTISED BY CONGREGATIONS

D0064171

EDITED BY ANDRÉ BIRMELÉ

World Council of Churches, Geneva

ISBN 2-8254-0796-8
Printed in Switzerland

CONTENTS

PREFACE

The report presented here is the final report of a four-year study project suggested by the Sixth Assembly of the Lutheran World Federation in Dar-es-Salaam in 1977 and carried out by the Institute for Ecumenical Research in Strasbourg.

The original aim of this study was to define the contribution which ecumenical endeavours and experiences on the local level can have for interconfessional dialogues carried out on various levels of church life. Questions specific to the local level should be addressed and discussed in such a manner as to make possible a better relationship between the ecumenism experienced in the local parishes and the bilateral and multilateral theological dialogues. The question which has arisen throughout the ecumenical movement concerning the reception of the results of previous dialogues can only be answered if the ecumenical situation "on the local level" is carefully taken into consideration. At the same time one must be aware of the difficulty of the concept "local", especially when used with regard to ecclesial entities (local church, local parish etc.). In our study we do not use this concept in a technical sense, but simply in order to describe the area where Christians live with one another in communities or other groups.

Execution of the study

The first stage of the study project was an appraisal of what happens, on the local level, from the point of view of ecumenism. Thus groups, parishes and Christians of the most diverse confessional and geographical origins were visited or requested by letter to describe in a situation report their efforts towards unity. In view of a lack of ecumenical interest in many places, we have deliberately concentrated on the situations where, on the local level, the separation between the churches is felt and thus there is a joint attempt to overcome this separation. Some of the authors of the reports were active lay people and others were pastors and priests. We felt it important not to receive general statements on ecumenism from any particular church, but rather reports from quite concrete local situations, written by those who were personally involved. It was of course not possible to collect all local experiences. This was not only due to the multiplicity of situations, but also to the special difficulties which distinguish the many groups. Whereas some groups gladly explained their situation, others shunned all forms of publicity for fear of reactions, not least from church authorities. Some requested highly confidential treatment of their material, while others wished to remain anonymous. In order to respect these wishes, in our final report we have quoted extracts from the situation reports providing information only regarding their country of origin.

Through situation reports, many personal contacts, contributions by participants at various meetings, visits of local or regional groups, follow-up enquiries, etc., we obtained a colourful cross-section from very different situations. This cross-section ranged from informal "basic groups", through active ecumenical parish circles, ecumenical education in schools, or youth work to traditional village or town parishes. We have also attempted to gain as wide a geographical spectrum as possible, and have received important contributions from older and newer churches from all continents.

A first and provisional evaluation of the results of the study led to the publication of an interim report in the winter of 1980-81. This first report was intended to elicit reactions and comments and to provide the possibility for corrections and changes of emphasis. We received a great deal of information and additional situation reports. We were also invited to discussions and could thus substantially broaden our background of information.

At the same time we submitted our results to the judgment of experts who had a wealth of ecumenical experience. Together with possibilities which presented themselves at scholarly colloquia (e.g. in the Societas Oecumenica), two consultations sponsored by the Institute which we should mention in particular were devoted exclusively to this study project. The first was held in June 1981 near Strasbourg and involved representatives of different confessional origins from North and South America and Europe. The second consultation took place in Pematangsiantar, Indonesia, where representatives from various churches in Asia and Africa were brought together. Both consultations provided impulses which were taken up and incorporated in the present final report. We are indebted to all consultation participants and would like to thank in particular the lecturers, Prof. Dr G. Sauter (FRG), Dr K. Schmidt (FRG), Prof.

Dr Johnson (USA), Rev. K. McDonnell (USA), Dr Choong Chee Pang (Singapore), Dr B.H. Jackayya (India), and Dr A. Sitompul (Indonesia). They all participated substantially in this report through their contributions and their careful consideration of the interim results. The material from these consultations and all of the study project material are kept at the Strasbourg Institute and may be consulted there.

Finally, reference must be made to previous studies and already existing material which we were able to use in our study and which was a great help to us, such as the LWF's Methodology Study (1977), the work of the ecumenical institutes of Utrecht and Münster, the Ökumenische Zentrale Frankfurt, etc.

The final report

The final report of the study is divided into five chapters:

I. Ecumenical motivation on the local level
II. The role of pastors and priests in local ecumenism
III. Concepts of unity on the local level
IV. The significance of doctrinal questions on the local level
V. The influence of non-doctrinal factors.

According to the majority of the reports, these are the points which decisively determine local ecumenism, although it is possible that the emphasis may differ from case to case. In order to do justice to the abundance of observations and points of view, we have attempted, within these chapters, to distinguish and arrange the data more exactly. Since, however, each local situation is characterized by factors specific to that particular place, factors which can, moreover, change very quickly, the individual observations of this study clearly do not apply to each local area. In the colourful ecumenical diversity contrary examples can be brought forward against each of the basic tendencies that we have ascertained. Nevertheless we think we have presented, all things considered, a true picture of the local ecumenical situation.

Our report is first of all simply an account of what happens ecumenically on the local level. At the same time, however, we wanted to go beyond a mere description by analyzing and evaluating the data. One particular question repeatedly concerned us — and still remains unresolved: on the basis of these observations, how far is it possible to give advice and help which could be the starting points for future efforts towards ecumenism on the local level? Of course some such insights can be deduced from this study without difficulty. For the careful reader they are to a certain extent evident, e.g. a more thorough education for pastors in ecumenical matters, the need for better ecumenical information and communication, etc. However, the majority of the questions raised cannot be answered with "ecumenical recipes". It occurred to us again and again that the basic questions of local ecumenism are very often not specifically "ecumenical" questions: they often relate to the *ecumenical aspect* of questions and tensions which in general influence the life of every Christian community on the local level — tensions between the "lived" community and the institution, between the doctrine of the church and what is believed on the local level, between church and social life, or questions as to the role and task of the local clergy, questions about the understanding of the church, the task of the Christian, etc. It was not the goal of our study to discuss these basic questions even in an introductory manner. Proceeding from ecumenical presuppositions we came across these questions, and have attempted to analyze and clarify the consequences for local ecumenism which arise from them. Merely to make "ecumenical recommendations" would not get us anywhere. There will only be changes in local ecumenism if the basic questions which lie behind it are taken into consideration.

It will probably be noticed that during the course of this study we appear to have avoided the questions posed at the outset. The results of the study extend beyond the original question of the contribution of local ecumenism to interconfessional dialogues, and deal with the problem of local ecumenism in a more comprehensive sense. We believe, however, that we have nevertheless been able to remain true to our task. For fruitful work in ecumenical dialogues it is of great importance to have as extensive an insight as possible into what happens in those places where the results of these dialogues are expected to be translated into practice. On the other hand, it seemed important to us to hold up as broad a mirror as possible to Christians on the local level in their ecumenical endeavours. The question of whether and where this mirror reflects a distorted picture has to be left to the judgment of Christians living on the local level. We hope, however, that the picture we present will contribute to and stimulate critical reflection about the particular situation on the local level and that it will lead to new beginnings and new courage for the ecumenical task.

The results of our study should be passed on to local communities and groups, to church leadership bodies, to those who are responsible for ecumenical dialogues, to ecumenical groups and organizations. The task should be to consider the points raised here and to seek possibilities for the fulfilment of the ecumenical mandate — especially on the local level — better than before.

Our study project has been brought to a close only temporarily. We shall therefore be grateful for any further insights, reflections or proposals. With the help of new contributions we hope to resume this study at a later date and to be able to carry forward and refine our observations, analyses and proposals. (Contributions should be sent to the Institute for Ecumenical Research, 8 rue Gustave-Klotz, 67000 Strasbourg, France.)

To conclude, we would like to thank all those who made this study possible through their reports, contributions, comments and reactions; and those who will contribute to it in the future. Our special thanks go to those who, although not on the Institute staff, were intensely involved in the study at certain stages. Apart from the lecturers at the consultations, we would especially like to mention Dr M. Weyerstall, Secretary of the Coordinating Committee of the Leuenberg Doctrinal Discussions in Europe, and Dr A. Ahlbrecht, editor of the periodical *Ökumene am Ort*.

André Birmelé, Sutan Hutagalung, Carter Lindberg,
Per Lønning, Harding Meyer and Vilmos Vajta

Strasbourg, Whitsuntide 1982

I. ECUMENICAL MOTIVATION ON THE LOCAL LEVEL

1. The desire for unity among Christians and churches throughout the world has received new life during our century. Dialogue between Christians and churches of different historical origins and cultural characters and the endeavours for unity on all levels of church life are increasingly evident. "Ecumenism" belongs to ecclesial life. This is also becoming more and more valid for the local level where Christians live close to one another in congregations and special groups.

Behind all this stand numerous and varied motivations.

A. Challenges of society

2. In many areas of life in a pluralistic society one meets Christians of other confessions. In experiencing the condition of being separated, one attempts to understand others and asks about the possibilities of Christian community.

3. The secularized or atheistic environment, where Christians are mostly in a minority, is a challenge to a common Christian witness. Only a Christianity speaking with one voice is credible in such a context.

> Students, apprentices, workers, intellectuals (doctors) from various churches and Christian groups pull together because of outside pressure, because one needs the other. (GDR)
> "May they all be one, that the world may know that they are all my disciples."
> The lack of unity among neighbouring Christians of various confessions, etc. endangers the credibility of the witness in every community and among those who are not Christians. (GDR)

4. In Asia or Africa where small Christian minorities often face strong majority communities practising other faiths, this challenge is particularly evident.

> Divided churches cause a good deal of anxiety. The old saying, "United we stand, divided we fall", may be prophetic for the church in Malaysia. The number of adherents of other faiths is increasing because of their

mission strategies and rich resources. In such circumstances, unless the churches are united, they will be steadily marginalized. (Malaysia)

The basic motives are the wish and desire of Christians in these places to bring about community between Christians living close to one another, and to provide an example of community to the society. (Indonesia)

Christians are ready to work together on joint actions or statements because it is beneficial to do so. Ecumenism in a minority context becomes a matter of survival for all Christians: "If we do not hang together, we shall all be hanged separately." This point is very significant for the understanding of ecumenism in Asia. It is realistic and pragmatic. (Singapore)

5. Concrete social, ethical or political problems with which one is confronted in daily life in society are also the rationale for joint actions between Christians of different origins, which transcend prevailing confessional boundaries.

> ...joint action for peace, deliberations on nuclear energy,... joint care for the elderly. (FRG)
> ...attempts to improve life on the local level. (France)

Therefore even small opportunities are important.

> A certain integration results from joint actions: festivities involving children and families... collection of used paper. (FRG)

6. The task of creating and consolidating a new state (nation-building) is understood and perceived by the churches in many parts of the world as an ecumenical task in which they participate together. In many Asian and African countries the Christian churches belong to movements which can act in a decisive way in the creation of a new society which goes beyond traditional, local boundaries. Solutions are sought jointly, also in emergency situations (such as natural catastrophes).

> "Fellowship" groups of Christian doctors and lawyers from all churches meet and discuss their professions in the light of their faith. The Christian Medical Fellowship and the Christian Lawyers' Fellowship have had considerable influence upon the development of legislation concerning abortion and divorce. (Singapore)
> One should also not overlook the continuing attempts by the governments towards national unity and for nation-building and their relationship to the unity of the churches. (Indonesia)
> In case of national catastrophes people join together to help each other — regardless of religion, caste or denomination; building houses, providing clothes for the people and meeting other needs. There were many meetings where this was spoken of. (India)
> Lutherans and Catholics cooperated in the relief work after flood damage. There are joint relief services of both churches. (India)

7. Radio, TV, books and journals provide much information about other churches. Prejudices are reduced, new impressions gained. On the basis of more recent developments within the churches, their separation would appear in many places to be an outdated historical situation.

> We suddenly discovered that the Catholic Church was no longer what we had thought it was. Many things had changed in the last few years. This was the starting point for an initial discussion which was then followed by others. (FRG)
>
> We must communicate clearly to Protestants that the Roman Catholic Church no longer considers Martin Luther as a devil but accepts him as a religious man. (India)

8. Personal experience (family gatherings, travel, etc.) leads to acquaintance with the praxis and piety of other parish communities, raises new questions and presses for their solutions. Here the numerous cases of interdenominational marriages are a particularly important factor.

> It is in the increasing number of mixed marriages that the confessional separation can be felt most directly. Even if the majority of mixed marriage partners decide for one church in the interest of the religious education of their children, they nevertheless often express the desire for as many ecumenical events as possible.
>
> In other instances there are often very concrete, local factors which lead to joint activity. The churches must for instance take up the discussion and agree amongst themselves when they want to submit their propositions for a new timetable in the schools (school reform). It would no longer be understood today if the confessional churches wanted to undertake separate activities with regard to many social problems and enquiries. (Switzerland)
>
> Mutual acquaintance, e.g. attending the worship service of another confession, is more effective in breaking down historical prejudices than theoretical information, the results of ecumenical dialogues on a higher level being passed down via the pastor. (GDR)

9. Such ecumenical motivation is effective in many places, even if sometimes unarticulated. It is the result of local conditions, new knowledge and new understandings of each other, new personal and community experiences or changes in familiar situations. Yet these social factors are only one aspect of ecumenical motivation.

B. Hope for the renewal of the church
10. The strongest ecumenical motivation for many Christians who seriously want to live their faith is the renewal of the church. There are hopes for a general deepening and strengthening of Christian

faith and life from ecumenical endeavours, which of course will also touch the individual parish. People in many places are disappointed and depressed by the lack of spiritual life in their own church. They long for the renewal of a lived Christian faith.

> Ecumenical parish work on the local level is experienced as a "new spirit" which has suddenly taken hold of people and done something practical. (FRG)
> We live from the hope that one day one church will include all of us and will witness to Christ with one voice. That is what we are working for. (GDR)
> Local ecumenism points to the need for inner renewal and a deeper spiritual life in every church. (India)
> Therefore the best we can do today, in connection with ecumenism, is to bring renewal to the churches. (India)

11. This desire for the renewal of the church includes the longing for a strengthened, lived communion within the individual church and beyond its confessional boundaries.

> This time, besides the Evangelical and Catholic Churches, the Anglican Church, the Baptist community and the Catholic-Apostolic Church were also represented. Through spontaneous contributions and information from various churches our ecumenical horizon has been considerably broadened. The one outstanding experience of these days was the deep oneness in Christ, which developed into a wonderful community, in peace of heart, in patient listening to one another, in unanimity and mutual attentiveness. The understanding and love between us was expressed not only through words, but also in spontaneous songs and dances, in which young and old were joined together. (GDR)

12. Unity of the church and the common witnessing of the one faith should also help confer on the churches a new and stronger influence, and further their credibility in a world which seems for the most part to be able to survive without their contribution.

> The situation in the world around us necessarily calls for solidarity among parishes, which is represented by a united church. (GDR)

C. Ecumenism: a secondary concern?
13. These great ecumenical hopes however have not been realized in many local situations. What was expected did not come to pass. The hoped-for renewal through the ecumenical movement of the church and its life failed to appear.

> At the present time this renewal would not appear to be imminent. Our ecumenical working group can only count on small numbers. (FRG)

The local papers invariably translate "ecumenical movement" as "the church-union movement". Many people take this literally to mean an immediate attempt to unite all the divided churches. As a result many people with high expectations are then disillusioned. (India)

Of course these disappointments can be attributed to an unrealistic impatience. But this is not an adequate explanation.

14. The observation that ecumenical endeavours on a local level seem in general to have no central significance is a decisive one. Indeed in many places there is ecumenical "interest", but interest alone does not necessarily mean that the concern for the unity of the church is a common and central concern of parish work. Even where ecumenical concern does receive a certain approval it is mostly not understood as a necessary and constitutive element of parish life. This is manifested in the fact that, alongside many other groups (youth groups, adult groups, Bible societies, choirs, etc.), there is also an "ecumenical group" and it is believed that the ecumenical concern of the parish is met in this way. Where such a group does not exist, a serious lack is hardly felt. The unity of the church seems to be felt as a confessional concern, as a central point in the understanding of the church. ("I believe... in one holy church...") It may also happen that a parish feels so self-satisfied — that it already has so many activities and so many demands made on it — that ecumenical endeavours appear either superfluous or simply as an extra burden.

The worshipping community feels little need for joint worship services. Occasional ecumenical worship services (e.g. youth pilgrimages that have been held in various churches during the last years), joint worship services during the ecumenical prayer week, or ecumenical participation in the church elder day of the senior Protestant minister, are accepted benevolently by the parish. However, people feel most at home in the tradition of their own worship service. (GDR)

Unfortunately one must admit that ecumenical endeavours among the majority of laity and clergy are met with indifference — whether because they consider the search for unity as incidental in the life of the church, or are discouraged by the excuses and contradictions of the church authorities, or they consider it as an already solved problem — if not actual hostility from the few who hold tight to the past and fear the loss of certain privileges, and thus work against any progress in this area in the defence of a misunderstood confessional identity. (France)

Because our local Catholic community, ecumenically considered, is relatively lifeless, there are hardly any conflicts or subsequent reactions. (FRG)

The Catholic Church is so closed in on itself and so full of its own structural and spiritual life, that it can exist quite well without ecumenical contacts; as a result of its traditional majority, the Evangelical community is also not dependent on ecumenical contact. (GDR)

15. Ecumenical concern on the parish level remains in many cases the concern of individuals, or very small groups which often consist of Christians who are brought together through personal friendships or common interests or who have painfully experienced the separation of the church in their own lives. This is also valid for some mixed marriage couples, although the vast majority of such marriages only play a small role ecumenically as all too often they stand apart from church life.

> Sometimes on a parish level it is indeed frustrating when perhaps only 20-30 people from two Catholic and one Evangelical parishes come to the monthly ecumenical prayer meetings and sometimes not even the pastors appear. (Netherlands)
>
> There is only a very small group involved in an ecumenical life here — and that developed from a group of friends. The parishes participate only partially or not at all. They are in no way "against" it but neither are they for it. The same is true for church leaders; hence the Evangelical pastors repeatedly claimed that the Catholics were not interested in a genuine ecumenism, but as always only wanted "conversion" in the sense of "back to Rome". (FRG)
>
> Couples in mixed marriages play virtually no role in promoting ecumenical integration. Indeed, the majority would be overburdened under the circumstances (e.g. marked secularization, widespread instability of marriage and family, etc.). (FRG)

16. The observable ecumenical indifference is strengthened in many places by a certain fear of the loss of individual identity. In these situations the concept "ecumenical" has not been sufficiently thought out or clarified. It is misunderstood as the "surrendering of one's own identity" in favour of a new, not yet precisely defined identity in which all confessional churches will be dissolved. Such an unfortunately widespread picture of "ecumenism" is obstructive rather than liberating (see chapter III).

> ...ecumenical actions are often concentrated on programmes which are a goal in themselves. These ecumenical actions are regarded as expressions of fellowship in the Lord or as a way to exercise social responsibility. They are very seldom taken seriously as possibilities for the realization of a formal ecclesial fellowship. The mere proposal of a formal ecclesial fellowship is actually sufficient to keep people away from active participation in these programmes. (Singapore)

17. There is often a static understanding of one's own ecclesial life in the understandable and legitimate concern to keep one's independence and identity. Because of this, every change in ecclesial life, and even small shifts in self-understanding or questioning as a

result of contributions from other traditions, are understood all too quickly as loss of identity and are therefore rejected.

> On the whole I have the impression that there is indeed the readiness in both churches for practical cooperation on many concrete questions. Yet at the same time both churches want to maintain their individuality and their own life. This holds true also for the Reformed churches in the diaspora area which, as minority churches, want in particular to be understood as equal partners. (Switzerland)
> The majority of pastors and parish members believe that "ecumenism" means that we must sacrifice some of our teaching and our belief... We must sacrifice some of our good teachings. It will be problematic to share the possessions of the missions and institutions such as schools, colleges and hospitals. (India)

D. Ecumenical consciousness of those responsible for parishes

18. Clear ecumenical advances are only really to be seen on the level of the "core communities"; that is to say, engaged parish members, pastors, church leaders, those responsible for the parish religious education. The anticipation of a renewal of the church and the parish is at its most lively on this intermediate ecclesial level. It is here that much develops and is accomplished — from joint meetings, studies, and concrete actions in ethical, social and societal areas, to personal friendships. Here ecumenism is experienced as a great gain for the church in general and the individual parish in particular. The following testimony of a Catholic priest is representative of similar reports in which this is stressed:

> A pastor comes to mind... a companion of this time of discovery, this ecumenical springtime, who was completely illumined with grace. Roland T. died in 1972. We always found ourselves in complete pastoral fellowship. I had given him a small icon of the Last Supper. It went with him during his last illness. I accompanied him on his last journey to the cemetery and gave thanks for his life. In loyalty and respect to our ecclesial disciplines we could never take holy communion together. We were just at the threshold of the adventure of unity. Nevertheless I must say that that which I experienced in depth with men and women of Roland T.'s spiritual quality already belongs to the mystery of the communion of saints, to the church of tomorrow, which is not as yet clearly revealed. (France)

19. However, only a few of these positive impulses show through on most local levels. Although it may not appear expressly formulated in any of the situation reports, it can still be seen that in the area of ecumenical endeavours the situation in the everyday life of the church is not only of no help but in some cases may even be a hindrance.

E. Ecumenical "basis groups"

20. Less is heard these days concerning the so-called ecumenical "basis groups" which arose in so many areas. A careful distinction must be made between these groups.

21. On the one hand, there are groups which consciously desire to live outside the church and "no longer expect anything from the church", as was said in a report from Denmark. They develop independently and do not seek any relationship with already existing ecclesial institutions. They attempt to remain "anonymous" and for this reason have no true "impact".

22. Other groups, however, want consciously to have an influence on the traditional local parishes even if this often meets only with small success. They want to be the catalyst for new life. This is particularly valid for groups closely connected to the charismatic movement. Some of their concerns have occasionally been fulfilled, but here too there is still the danger of disappointment.

> We wanted consciously to have an influence within our respective churches; we also succeeded here and there in bringing in some contributions of our renewal movements; however, we unfortunately had to acknowledge that the life and structure of our parishes and churches are by no means as open as we had believed. (Netherlands)

F. Implicit ecumenism

23. However, "local ecumenism" is not only to be measured by the activities that take place between different churches. There is also a static, only partly perceivable, ecumenical openness and character of parish work, a kind of "implicit ecumenism", expressed through proclamation and teaching, mutual intercession and new common forms of spirituality, the use of songs, spiritual examples and texts from other confessions. This acceptance of elements from other Christian confessions is an essential form of ecumenical openness, particularly for parishes that have no partners of different confessions in their area.

> Hymns by Luther were included in the new edition of our hymnal. In this way all our (Catholic) parishes have access to a spiritual heritage which was unknown to them until now. (Alsace/France)
>
> Our pastor (Evangelical) often prays in the worship service with the words of the Dutch Catholic Oosterhuis. (FRG)
>
> For more than a year now we have held an early morning service from 5.30 to 6.00 every day of the week. This service consists of prayer, song and sermon. It attracts people from all the churches in the area. (Indonesia)

II. THE ROLE OF PASTORS AND PRIESTS IN LOCAL ECUMENISM

1. "Local ecumenism" depends to a great extent on the local clergy, the priests and pastors of the area. This statement may provoke questions and objections: should not the parish itself as a whole and not only the pastors be concerned about the unity of the church on the local level? The Lord of the church — not the priests — is the centre of its unity. Such objections certainly have their justification, but they should not be raised too hastily. The empirical evidence shows that local ecumenism is heavily dependent on the attitude and the personal engagement of the local clergy and pastoral co-workers. Whether desirable or not, it is nevertheless clear that in many places ecumenical work has developed only because of the initiatives, efforts and personal engagement of the local clergy.

A. What is expected of the local clergy

2. There is a singular concentration on the question of ministry at the local level too, though it is expressed there differently from formal theological interchurch dialogues. The understanding of the office of pastor as exercised in the parish, in society and within one and the same church, has a decisive influence on local ecumenism. There can of course be quite a discrepancy between the pastor's understanding of his office of ministry and the understanding of the pastoral office among others.

3. The pastors are assigned a key function by their parishes. Even the pastors who take a lively interest in the initiatives of their parishioners and in the priesthood of all the baptized can hardly avoid the expectations others have of them. In many situations, especially in Asian and African churches, the pastor is considered as the one who has "spiritual and theological knowledge". Therefore the initiatives taken up by the laity are continually dependent on the consent and cooperation of the pastors, even for the sake of their credibility within the parish itself. Non-participation by the local clergy is quickly seen as disapproval, even where this is not the case.

We always try to involve the local pastors in the long run for anything we undertake without them is fruitless. (Denmark)

In any case it is necessary to have committed pastors taking part, for nothing works if the pastors are against it. (FRG)

4. This expectation does not only exist in the parishes where the local clergy fulfill the service of ministry. Even in the ecumenical endeavours between confessionally different parishes the perspective always concentrates on the person of the local clergy. It seems to be through them that the other confessions are defined. They are regarded as their representative, almost their "expression".

5. This is confirmed when one considers in general people's expectations of the local clergy in societal life. The general change in the ecclesial and social situation has resulted in the person of the pastor being increasingly understood, outside the parish, in social and political life, as the visible representative of the church. It means that the credibility of the Christian message and of ecumenical endeavours can be determined by the image of the pastor. This is strengthened by the fact that very often pastors have an ecumenical function when they must appear outside the life of the parish in public social life (cf. comments on the significance of non-doctrinal factors, see chapter V). A similar role is imposed on them also in the case of services and official functions and by those people who only have occasional contacts with the church. The expectations of these ecclesial "outsiders" render local ecumenism even more dependent upon the person of the pastor.

B. The self-understanding of the bearer of the office of ministry

6. The self-understanding of pastors and priests, as well as their place within society, has become problematic in our day. The ministry of the local clergy no longer appears to be legitimated by their representing an institution whose public position is based on centuries-old history. This problematic extends far beyond the particular ecumenical question, though it does have some important consequences for ecumenical matters. It influences the whole self-understanding and exercise of the office of ministry and thereby also ecumenical events on the local level.

7. Pastors also come under the influence of the attitude which expects achievement and success. Even if it does not reach the point where the local pastors measure and justify their activity by the criterion of success, he or she is nevertheless always in danger of encouraging those things which, at least for the moment, seem to

promise greater success than others. Since instruction in doctrine and faith is no longer requested by the majority of people, the local clergy easily accept the role of an "enabler". Thus highly visible ecumenical "spectaculars" are often given preference over the more laborious ecumenical spadework. The fear of failure can easily lead to a striving for ecumenical sensationalism, which hardly brings lasting results.

8. This usually does not correspond to the basic intentions of the pastors themselves. First of all from ecumenism he or she hopes to promote a revival and deepening of parish life as other confessions contain elements which are positive and can be useful for the life of one's own parish. The pastor would be prepared to follow the more difficult path of contributing to ecumenism by taking one small step at a time. However, the already-mentioned expectations of pastors and the need to be able to show "success" force them to follow a different path. The local clergy become ecumenical "animators", and important and noticeable ecumenical initiatives are expected from them which, if possible, should make the headlines.

9. The pastors very often attempt to fulfill this role which is assigned to them, and conform so much to it that they become convinced that the life of the local parish and efforts towards unity are totally dependent on them. This can develop to such an extent that an ecumenical initiative which bypasses the pastors may appear to them as a loss of authority.

10. The question of priorities which one sets for oneself is also of great significance. The ecumenical task is seen by some as lacking in priority; it is seen as an additional workload and is therefore not given much attention. For others the opposite view is valid; these pastors invest much time and energy in this task, even when the fruits do not correspond to the efforts.

11. The local clergy's understanding of their ecumenical task, as well as the various ecumenical expectations made of them, inevitably leads to the extensive dependency of local ecumenical efforts on the person of the local pastor. This goes so far that a change of pastor for a parish can mean a sudden change in the ecumenical attitude of the parish. If a pastor who is strongly motivated ecumenically is followed by a more cautious colleague, or vice-versa, it is often possible to observe the parish changing its ecumenical orientation within a very short time.

Until two years ago we had a relatively lively ecumenical discussion group. Then suddenly the Evangelical superintendent died and then, even more suddenly, his replacement also died. On the Catholic side, there was a change of the pastor; he was followed by a neighbouring priest who still had to care for his old parish. On the Evangelical side the team... is again complete, but the workload on the Catholic side and the difficulties of beginning the new position on the Evangelical side, have paralyzed the old ecumenical work. And all this took place against the background of the election of a new mayor, in which the Social Democratic Party (SPD) used, in part, Protestant confessional arguments, thus causing, on the Catholic side, the old diaspora type confessionalism to become virulent once again. (FRG)

While my predecessors and pastoral colleagues disregarded faith questions with regard to the Catholic Church, I urged, from the beginning, that since there has been religious development on both sides since the Reformation, the two faiths should be freshly compared. I urged this as a position from which mutually responsible and public witness and service to contemporary society, though not however mutual religious activity, could begin. I think this "indifference" concealed a resistance to Catholic activities, which were seen as designed to promote the public significance of the Catholic Church under the pretext of ecumenism. My pastoral colleagues were included to avoid a conflict and simply tolerated this so-called "ecumenism". And in this way they were not seriously opposed by the church members. (FRG)

12. The personal relationship of the pastors is also always very important. Personal tensions and mistrust are characteristic of many local situations. If this is the case between the pastors of different confessions, then almost always the result is the breaking off of relations and the failure of ecumenical endeavours. On the other hand sympathy or friendliness between the clergy who represent Christian churches on the local level can lead to good understanding and cooperation also among the parishes. Such good relationships can lead to much which was often previously unthinkable on a local level. In particular situations (e.g. in relation to the free churches) ecumenism is on the whole only possible in virtue of such a personal relationship of trust. If however ecumenical cooperation on the local level is too exclusively dependent on the personal relationship of the ministers, this can also bring about serious dangers. This raises the question of what role such personal relationships *could* play in the building up of the church on the local level. In any case the personal relations between the clergy of the different confessions on the local level is of great significance. But it depends more on the personalities involved than on theological reflection, and this is a "random" factor.

It is not to be denied that personal sympathies between pastors can considerably further cooperation between two parishes. In our case none of the ministers had ever in the past had any markedly bad experience with other confessions, which could have given rise to prejudices or mistrust. Psychologically, this is a question on both sides concerning "people" who are able to trust and who in difficult situations within their own field would consciously seek the advice and comfort of colleagues in other confessions. (FRG)

C. The pastor's ecumenical function as mediator and translator

13. The pastor's ecumenical function as mediator and translator is decisive for local ecumenism. There is no doubt that the pastor has a key position in the communication process between local ecumenism and other levels of ecclesial life where there is a grappling with ecumenical-theological questions, or where ecumenical-ecclesial decisions are encountered.

14. The function of pastors first of all concerns the passing on of information about ecumenical developments and insights. Although there are complaints in some situation reports about the lack of information or too selective a passing on of information on the local level, it would appear that in many places the ministers try to keep their parishes well informed. This holds true for churches in Europe and North America as well as Asian and African churches where the ministers are the sole source of information for local parishes.

> The local ministers do not pass on the results of the ecumenical, theological agreement and official interchurch agreements to their parishes. Our information comes only from church newspapers. (FRG)
>
> Our minister does try, but unfortunately the response to invitations to such meetings of adult theological education is relatively weak. (FRG)

15. The ecumenical function of mediating and translating is a double task: on the one hand the results of translocal ecumenical (regional, national, international) dialogues should be made available at the local level; on the other hand, the local results should at least be given recognition on the "higher" levels, so that ecumenical endeavours on all levels could be mutually stimulated.

16. This double task is certainly not only the task of the local pastor. Therefore it would be wrong to make only the local ministers responsible for the failure of connection between the various levels of church life. Here one should expect help first from church leadership, ecumenical lecturers and world organizations and from interconfessional dialogues. This is a task of the whole church and must therefore be taken seriously by everyone. However it would be just as wrong to relativize or even deny the responsibility of the local pastors on this point. What is to be done?

17. The results of interconfessional discussion on a level higher than that of the parish are the product of a process of reflection and study by an ecumenical group. For these results to be received on the local level it is crucial that every process should to a certain extent already be worked out. The results of a dialogue can only be received when a local parish subsequently carries them out, engages in its process of learning and in this way adopts such results.

18. Of course in many local situations transregional consensus texts are recognized or discussed. However the authority and binding forces of such texts often remain unclear. There are only very few examples of parishes or parish groups which duplicate the whole thought and learning process of the development of a text and which subsequently make an attempt really to appropriate the contents. The local pastors here have a decisive ecumenical and hermeneutical task.

19. If this task of the local clergy is only seldom recognized and undertaken, one must recall the expectations people have of the local pastor (cf. chapter II/A). The "behaviour" of pastors, their active work and not so much their "teaching", is called into question. For this reason many pastors do not see the need for integrating into their teaching the ecumenical-hermeneutical task. Indeed there is also a lack of hermeneutical aids, of supplementary texts to the dialogues, which should be provided by the international dialogues themselves or by church leadership in order to help the pastors in their task.

20. On the other hand, it is also the task of the local clergy to help make local efforts fruitful for regional and transregional endeavours. It is important for local ecumenical events to be analyzed, so that their theological content and implications become clear and valid, not only for one place but for local ecumenism in general. Only then can the local event be of real importance for church life as a whole and for comprehensive dialogues between churches. This task also is not just the task of the local clergy, but as they know and understand the local situation best, they must of course play an important role in this process.

21. Unfortunately this mediation from local to translocal ecumenical levels occurs only in exceptional cases. This ecumenical-hermeneutical task is made more difficult by an "egoistical", self-satisfied understanding of the parish, especially in many Protestant churches. As the church — in the mind of the parish member as well — is continually reduced to the local parish, the need for serious consideration of questions, events and concerns which transcend the local level is often not registered. In this respect, the Roman Catholic

Church, where the dimension of catholicity and universality of the church is more clearly perceived — even by the parishioner — seems to have found a more favourable starting point.

22. This task of mediation between various levels of ecclesial life is not only an ecumenical question. It appears also in other areas of ecclesial life. However in ecumenics this task has a particular urgency precisely because in many places it is not recognized at all, or seen as an extra. Hence there is a growing danger that local and trans-local ecumenical endeavours will be increasingly separated from each other, thus endangering the unity of the ecumenical movement.

23. It is striking that this important ecumenical-hermeneutical task of the clergy was hardly dealt with in the situation reports, even if the role of the pastor on the local level was frequently emphasized. Without doubt this shows the urgent need to re-evaluate the office of ministry and the role of the pastor. In particular this shows the obvious deficiencies in the ecumenical-theological education of pastors and students. It is important to examine how the various pastoral education programmes could be made more suitable in terms of the demands of ecumenical work.

III. CONCEPTS OF UNITY
ON THE LOCAL LEVEL

1. The conceptions one has of the unity to be attained or even regained also play an important role on the local ecumenical level. It is often here that the decision for ecumenical motivation and ecumenical engagement is taken. Even the type and the manner of work towards the realization of unity are necessarily determined by the concepts which one has of the unity that is sought.

2. It would of course be fruitless to look for properly formed "concepts of unity" at the local level, more or less corresponding to those which have developed in the interchurch dialogues and in ecumenical-theological discussions of models and concepts of unity. Here it is more a question of the existence of still unreflected concepts or tendencies and fears. On this level they have not yet taken shape as concepts of unity in the stricter sense, but they are still effective.

A. The relation between unity and diversity

3. One of the most important points of view in the question of concepts of unity is how one sees the relation of unity and diversity. It is clear that unity cannot be realized if the existing differences are simply ignored. The question is: to what extent would the removal of differences be required in order to attain unity? Is every difference felt to be divisive or can differences also be seen in another way?

4. Almost instinctively, difference is experienced as strange, alienating and divisive. "Candles on the altar!" exclaimed a scandalized Swiss Reformed woman after her first visit to a Lutheran service, and added with a sense of definite rejection, "that's Catholic!" This same attitude is evident where there is the feeling that for the sake of unity one should ignore already existing differences, that they should be tolerated or simply passed over in silence with the assertion: "In the end, we all have the same God." In short, differences are feared and unwanted, since people can see them only as alienating and divisive.

5. This almost instinctive resistance to every form of difference and, as a result, the unreflective inclination to think of unity as uniformity, must be taken account of at the local level.

6. Such a basic attitude endangers and even blocks ecumenical engagement and ecumenical motivation. People who can only see differences as alienating and divisive, and as a result think of unity only as the elimination of every difference, will be forced, when they no longer hang on to the naive hope of the "conversion" of others to their own conviction and church, to conclude that the realization of unity signifies a basic surrender of their own ecclesial or confessional identity. And when they cannot accept this, they feel obliged to reject all ecumenical endeavours.

7. On the local level such rejection very often shows itself in the form of accusing others of using ecumenism only as a pretext for leading people towards (or back) to one's own church. In other words, the familiar criticism that others are using ecumenism for denominational gain and the ecumenical rejections based on this result from the inability to think of unity as other than uniformity and the surrender of present identity.

B. Positive evaluation of diversity

8. It is interesting and important to see that the basic attitude of instinctive rejection of difference disappears in proportion to the extent to which ecumenical interest arises, becomes concrete and grows stronger.

9. In response to the question as to whether diversity in spiritual forms of life can only be alienating or whether it could stimulate ecumenical discussion, the reports tend to give differing answers. This shows that on the level of a "mature" Christianity and an already formed ecumenical engagement, there is the development of an emphatically positive understanding of diversity; where these elements are lacking, there is a negative judgment of diversity.

> For Christians who understand themselves through the Holy Spirit as free and mature, the diversity of forms of piety is indescribably positive. ...For immature Christians its effect is "alienating". (FRG)
>
> The diversity of spiritual forms of life is experienced as predominantly enriching. The more intensive the cooperation, the better the understanding... (GDR)
>
> Among the majority of people, the confessions live side by side. For those who are ecumenically interested, (the diversity is) enriching. (FRG)
>
> It (i.e. diversity) stimulates ecumenical discussion and leads to deeper understanding — if it can be openly discussed. (USA)

From the moment when one starts to be concerned with others, diversity has never had an alienating effect, but is greatly stimulating and enlivening. (FRG)

10. The positive evaluation of diversity thus does not appear where ecumenical interest is superficial. The affirmation of diversity is therefore not, as clearly seen in the responses, a resigned "yes"; not a "yes" to peaceful but in the end divided coexistence of churches and confessions. It has the character of a stimulating and liberating spiritual "discovery", which suggests a community of lively exchanges and mutual learning, of giving and receiving.

11. Of course, this insight or this "discovery" of the positive value of diversity is not reached without opposition.

— This understanding of unity has its effect mainly in the sense of transcending diversity, the diversity of origins and the conceptions of those not ecumenically engaged or those who are slightly or not at all accustomed to being influenced by dialogue with others.

— There are perceptible difficulties in articulating, and explaining to oneself and others, those differences which are primarily experiential and have an intrinsic, spiritual legitimacy. Therefore there is need for some ability to make theological judgments in addition to having a living faith and an engaged ecumenical attitude, which is not and does not need to be the proprium of local ecumenism.

— Now it appears to be exactly here that there is the impression of being let down by the clergy and above all by the ecclesial leadership, indeed not only being left in the lurch, but often even hindered.

After the experience that the ecclesial leadership of all confessions did not go along this way (i.e. the way of discovering the spiritual substance of the others and the experience that diversity acts as a stimulant) one becomes resigned... What is experienced from the side of the clergy and the hierarchy is that every difference (Mariology, intercessions for the dead, justification by faith alone) are stressed so often that engagement with them on the local level is already hindered and does not occur. Instead it would be important that opportunity and freedom be given to recognize and articulate the legitimacy of differences. (France)

C. Features of a picture of unity

12. To what extent are there now already on the local level features of an understanding of unity which correspond to this experience and this concept? Of course, as already mentioned, there can be no talk

of proper "concepts of unity". However, in those places where a certain ecumenical experience exists, certain inclinations and disinclinations appear which together point in a certain direction.

13. The aim is apparently not to get rid of or to level all the differences. The point of departure is the awareness of the basic experience and the conviction arising from this that one, together with others, belongs to Christ. This basic experience occurs despite and in the face of present differences. That is not to say that these diversities are therefore invalid or harmless. It is known that it is necessary to deal with them and to attempt to come to terms with them in light of the basic experience and to solve the problems. A simple removal of the differences however is not the right solution to the problem.

14. On the local level there seems to exist an aversion to the merging of the institutional churches. The reasons and motives for this may of course be very varied: a general aversion to and a mistrust of all institutions as such and general anti-ecumenical tendencies may strengthen the conviction of the ecumenically committed that institutional merger is not an adequate realization of ecumenical communion.

15. Instead of wanting to attain unity through the abolition of all differences and instead of understanding ecclesial unity in terms of the merger of institutions, supporters and representatives of local ecumenism favour an idea of community. It is akin to the idea of the "family". That is, on the basis of a constitutive union or commonality, one understands oneself to be in the "family" — the family understood as a trustworthy and committed community — and can accept the differences of the individual members, as long as these differences do not question the basic unity or break up the family.

D. The binding character and universal dimension of community

16. This way of understanding unity and community of course also contains dangerous elements. These tend primarily in the following direction: within the bounds of such concepts of unity one may slight the obligatory character of ecclesial and Christian community, and rest content with a relatively lax realization of "community". That happens when there is all too much readiness to tolerate, without deeper consideration, the existing differences instead of giving account of the extent to which they hinder true community, and this must be dealt with. Certain observations lead one to ask whether ecumenical endeavours on the local level do not also occasionally stand in such danger.

17. Ecumenical cooperation and lived ecumenical community often are limited to specific occasions and times in the life of the individual or the local parish — weddings, baptisms, worship services on special holidays or festivals during the year, consecrations and similar occasions, annual prayer weeks, women's world day of prayer, etc. There is a lack of local ecumenism in "everyday" life and therefore it does not penetrate parish self-understanding and parish life. Of course clear limits are set to a stronger ecumenical penetration of our church life at the moment as a result of the state of ecumenical dialogues, because of still existing prejudices and of ecclesial statements. On the local level these limits cannot simply be overstepped. Yet the question needs to be asked as to whether, on the local level, such a lack is indeed felt as a lack, or whether there is not the tendency to be satisfied with "ceremonial ecumenism".

> The local conception of ecumenism is usually programme-oriented (sports, community celebrations, etc.) with little long-range vision for further ecclesial unity. Partly this is due to a wholesome enjoyment of the current programmes. (Indonesia)

18. Also forms of worship which include the celebration of holy communion, so-called "ecumenical weddings", and joint worship services have developed in many places which reflect more the nature of "coexistence" than "mutuality".

> One pastor has the introductory liturgy together with the rite of confession, the other preaches the sermon. Each year they change. After the sermon both pastors together read the preface. Then the Catholic priest speaks the words of institution and the high prayer, and after that the Evangelical pastor speaks the words of institution; then there is a joint Lord's Prayer and joint invitation to receive the sacrament at the altar. At this the Catholics go to their priest to receive communion, while at the same time the Evangelicals go to their pastor. The giving of thanks, prayer of intercession and blessing are again jointly spoken. (Austria)
>
> There is often a similar pattern for "ecumenical weddings": the pastor of the church where the wedding is to be held asks the marriage questions and hands over the ring. The marriage and the blessing of the pair are taken in turn by both pastors. Only twice so far has a wedding mass been asked for. As on both occasions this affected Catholic churches, we proceeded (in the following way): After the marriage ceremony the Catholics received the sacrament at the side altar of Mary, the Protestants at the side altar of the Apostles simultaneously and then they returned to the main altar for the closing prayer. (Austria)

19. It would be a mistake merely to criticize such attempts and to advise against them for the reason that they might appear as ecumenical window-dressing and are therefore more a demonstration

of division than of community. It is precisely on the local level that there is a need for concrete and visible expression of community. It is therefore important and legitimate that the community should "celebrate" even such incomplete common life as a gift and an achievement, and that this celebration should be made symbolically visible. Criticism is justified where, on the basis of a certain understanding of unity, such evidence of community is considered as sufficient and one no longer feels that — as seen in one of the reports — here at the same time "the whole agony of separation becomes visible". (FRG)

20. Local ecumenism is in danger of overlooking the comprehensive, universal dimension of the church and ecclesial unity. In part it depends on the participants' character and their understanding of the church of the partners involved, or on the relationships of the majority or minority on the local level. (The Catholics tend to give greater consideration to the universal dimension than the Protestants; minority groups because of their greater dependence need in particular the certainty of comprehensive belonging and community solidarity.)

21. However, an understanding of unity and community in which the element of mutual obligation is unsatisfactorily defined can only strengthen the danger of focusing on one's own parish and one's own place in endeavours towards ecumenical community. If local ecumenism is not to lead to new isolations, or even separations, the consciousness must be kept alive that the unity of the church is also binding beyond the local time and place.

IV. THE SIGNIFICANCE
OF DOCTRINAL QUESTIONS
ON THE LOCAL LEVEL

1. A first and superficial examination of the local situation leads to the conclusion that doctrinal questions have little significance for ecumenical work on the local level. Traditional points of controversy seem to be irrelevant since they are too distant from the reality of parish life.

> The traditional confessions and dogma have become questionable because they do not take into consideration the world in which we live today, because they do not respect a Christian's freedom of conscience and because they hinder ecumenical freedom. (FRG)
>
> In most cases doctrinal questions are of minimal interest for lay people on the local level. For the majority of lay people, doctrine does not seem important, as long as they can all be joined together in parish celebrations. (Indonesia)

A. The understanding of "doctrine"

2. This initial, hasty judgment has to be revised on closer consideration. The essential problem is not the "importance or nonimportance of doctrinal factors on the local level", but the understanding of the concept of doctrine. Here the discrepancy between the understanding of those responsible for the teaching office (church leaders, theologians, etc.) and that of parishioners, especially the ecumenically active ones, becomes evident. Even if the church leaders and theologians mean by doctrine the authenticity of contemporary preaching, loyalty to the apostolic heritage, historical continuity and consensus in the contemporary church, it is not understood in the same way at the local level. For those on the local level, "doctrine" is identical with defined, theologically formulated doctrines of normative character, comparable to a kind of law. These "doctrines" appear irrelevant because of their temporal and contextual distance from contemporary problems at the local level. They are felt to be stifling and detrimental to ecumenical endeavours. Nothing much is expected from these "doctrines", either for the

renewal of one's own parish or for the development of interchurch relationships.

3. The view that doctrine is meaningless for local ecumenism is a reflection of the conflict in the evaluation and understanding of ecclesial doctrine. It is possible to see here the basis for the "instinctive mistrust" with which local ecumenical groups view any kind of dogmatically motivated interference by translocal ecclesial authorities in the local ecumenical endeavours for unity. This appears to those on the local level to be a legalistic, administrative and bureaucratic interference, on the basis of church rules whose spiritual validity is rejected.

B. Practised community and doctrinal consensus

4. Ecumenical relationships on the local level are primarily oriented to cooperative activities (worship or socio-political action).

> The parishes are more interested in the possibilities of common praxis of the faith than in doctrinal agreement. (GDR)

5. As regards *church life* on the local level, the questions of joint worship services and full ecclesial and eucharistic community are the central points. Concrete activities are sought out, thought over, experimented with and manifested as examples in small or large ecumenical groups. Such groups want to have a common confession of faith and they hope it will be accepted as such by other levels of ecclesial life. In many cases, normative, dogmatic validity, which should apply beyond the local level to the level of the entire church, is demanded of it.

> The traditional controversial questions are insignificant today. On the contrary, the significant questions include divided worship services, separation at the Lord's Supper, non-recognition of ecumenical worship services as meeting the Sunday obligation. (Denmark)

6. In ecumenically active groups, questions of *Christian responsibility to the world and society* are often studied — such as questions concerning peace, justice, environmental protection, etc. At the same time the witness of the gospel of Jesus Christ, especially as it relates to the poor and rejected, is felt as an acute demand. The praxis-related relevance of Christ's teaching is emphasized especially with regard to joint Christian work.

7. Joint praxis would seem to be the decisive point. It has a normative character and in a certain sense becomes "doctrine". It is obviously not doctrine in the above traditional sense of a static legalistic

and theoretical system. It is here more of a kind of teaching in the original and true sense of the word — in words or deeds of evident truth — in no way merely theory. Common praxis can attain a normative character, orienting both thought and deed; and it is this praxis in the sense of "teaching" which becomes a concrete embodiment of truth. Therefore in the question of local ecumenism one can speak of praxis as implicit doctrine. Understood in this way, doctrine is of decisive importance on the local level.

8. The participation of the people of God in the churches' teaching mission is a legitimate concern which is being expressed once again through ecumenical experience. It raises the question of the changing relationship between praxis and doctrine and the significance of lived faith on the local level for the development of normative doctrine. This should be discussed more in ecumenical dialogue. However it must at the same time be clear that not every experience which results in ecumenical community has ecumenical legitimacy. The faith that is lived on the local level must be challenged by a vision responsible to the Christian faith in its largest dimensions.

C. The traditional doctrinal and disputed questions

9. The traditional doctrinal and disputed questions which have led to church division are considered in very different ways in the local context.

10. Where no ecumenical initiatives are taken up, these traditional, controversial questions are often in the foreground and are used to explain the existing divisions. It is possible to come across long out-of-date concerns which are no longer dealt with in the same way by the partners involved. Such controversial-theological "legitimations" of division witness not only to the historical burden of inter-ecclesial relations, but often also reflect certain social realities or power relations.

11. In other cases these differences are seen but are not taken as too important, since the plurality within their own ranks often shows greater differences than those which exist between confessions. Here, the traditional points of controversy are no longer alive in the consciousness of the parish, yet they can suddenly reappear or be raised when it is necessary to stop an ecumenical initiative on the local level (e.g. questions concerning the Pope, Mary, adoration of the saints, etc.).

The dogmatic questions on the local level are irrelevant. However if, for example, in the worship service bulletin there is mention of All Saints'

Indulgence of a Catholic parish, the Protestants are horrified. Also the question of the adoration of Mary or of the saints is shocking to some. (FRG)

...in spite of community gatherings for prayer and worship, it is rare to have a common celebration of the eucharist. Only rarely does the local congregation transcend its own historical situation to think of the wider church. However, when there is ecumenical progress, doctrinal issues do surface over baptism, the eucharist, etc. In Kerala, for example, intermarriage between members of the Orthodox and Mar Thoma churches is confronted by the Orthodox canon which permits marriage only on Sundays and Mondays. (India)

12. The situation is different, of course, in groups which are ecumenically active. Here such matters can be dealt with more objectively, to share information and to gain a better mutual understanding.

In the meantime in the Evangelical church leadership, the desire had been expressed to get to know the teachings of other confessions through discussion. Therefore meetings took place, at which other confessions presented their views. From the beginning it was possible to find a climate for discussion in which controversial questions could be discussed with great openness. (France)

13. The traditional doctrinal questions appear here in a different form and with different nuances. For example in the issue of the eucharist, the traditional question of Christ's real presence as such is only rarely asked, and the problem often arises of what to do with the left-over elements. The traditional doctrinal and controversial questions here are very real, even if differently formulated. However, their historical church-dividing character is no longer so acute.

D. The celebration of the eucharist

14. It is almost impossible to avoid the joint celebration of the eucharist as a decisive problem for local ecumenism where a Catholic partner is participating. The role played in this by traditional controversial questions is not that which is attributed to them in ecumenical dialogue on the higher level. The Lord's Supper is for many people the sign and expression of experienced ecumenical community. The common Christian ecumenical concern which brings the group together is seen as a distinguishing motive for joint celebration. Admonitions or even prohibition by church leadership bodies are incomprehensible for those on the local level. This causes many conflicts which those on the local level try hard to solve. In the face of ecclesial admonitions and prohibitions some advocate and practise

the "constructive disobedience" of a public invitation to a joint celebration of the eucharist. Others try interim solutions which often have an improvized and, in some cases, even a grotesque character — simultaneous celebrations by pastors at different altars, or at the same altar, on different sides or one after the other, reciprocal invitations where only the minister is absent, etc. Others finally forego all sacramental fellowship.

> Our ecumenical worship services are services of the word where until now no attempts have been made to undertake intercommunion. We pastors came to the understanding that we had no theological misgivings about intercommunion, but that out of respect for our parishioners would not practise it. It is presently being mutually considered whether in the future we should celebrate the eucharist at the same altar one after the other in the ecumenical services, or whether this would just serve to painfully emphasize the separation. For a long time now it has been impossible to prevent the young members in both parishes from taking communion in other parishes. We pastors tolerate this because a constructive disobedience is becoming evident with the help of which, hopefully, one day praxis will overtake theory — or else, the grass-roots will have a beneficial impact on the hierarchy. (FRG)
>
> The pastors are involved in the pulpit exchanges and not only preach in these services, but also undertake the intercessions. Without much enquiry the desire for common celebration of the eucharist became clear, where each minister brought his own elements and also administered them. (GDR)
>
> At a particular point in the worship the congregation divides, gathers around separate altars, repeats in unison such commonly held liturgical material as the acclamation ("Christ has died/Christ has risen/Christ will come again") and then, with each priest (Roman Catholic and Anglican) distributing, receives the bread and wine. There is no intercommunion as such. (USA)

E. The relationship to the church leadership

15. At the same time it is the Lord's Supper where the relationship of the local level to ecclesial boards of leadership becomes clear. Surprisingly, it can be seen that virtually all the ecclesial leadership — above all the Catholic — takes up the initiative for common celebration of the eucharist on the local level. Nevertheless, it is there that dialogue is most impossible. The presuppositions and aims on both sides are so entirely different that they talk past each other. (cf. chapter IV/A). The problem is dealt with by church leadership in the traditional dogmatic categories, and the arguments and testimonies from the local parishes find no place in the discussion. Individual parishes and ecumenical groups which experience the pain of separation on the local level feel it is a questioning of their faith when their

ecumenical experience is not taken into consideration or is rejected by higher bodies which do not have similar experiences.

16. The teaching office of the church must succeed in finding a way of rendering the basic apostolic heritage for church life in the parish understandable and meaningful in some other way than through the traditional dogmatic categories. Otherwise every attempt to impart the church's teaching at the local level will be rejected as an expression of ecclesial and hierarchical authoritarianism.

A clear renaissance of holy communion in the evangelical parish (in the meantime this has become a widely known phenomenon) with a reintroduction of the monthly mass, led to an increased desire for community with regard to this point. This culminated in a mutual invitation by the parishes to "their" Lord's Supper in 1979. The Evangelical parish attended the mass in St Fidelis on Easter Monday; the return visit of the Catholic parish was on Whit Monday to our eucharistic service, where nearly all the Catholics took communion. At this point the Diocese intervened and forbade the Catholic priest from participating in receiving communion. This barring "from above" has not yet been worked out. And not just here but in many places, the "local parish" is quite impatient with the caution of the ecclesial leadership. For the progress is felt to be a legitimate growth of community on the local level and people do not want this to be deprecated as hasty enthusiasm. (FRG)

17. The conflict between local ecumenical groups and the ecclesial authorities is particularly acute when the latter consider themselves as the undisputed bearers of the church's teaching and treat individual groups merely as those who are to listen and submit. The local parish does not desire any advice on normative doctrine, especially not in a thought-form and language which is incomprehensible to them. A decision made somewhere else will not automatically be accepted at the local level; it has to be validated in their own living community experience. There is the widespread suspicion that the motivation for church leadership in many of its interventions proceeds more from the desire to defend its power and governing position than from truth and doctrine. Even if this suspicion is not justified, it points to the need for church leadership to decide clearly between doctrinal questions on the one hand and ecclesial questions of order and discipline on the other hand.

Christians do suffer from the division of the churches... Many ordinary educated people have the impression that the church leaders are deliberately finding obstacles in the way to unity because they are unwilling to accept any changes in the present patterns of their authority and positions. But many lay people are hesitant to question this suspected attitude of the church leaders because of a sense of their own lack of expertise and experience in church matters. (India)

F. Inter-ecclesial dialogues and local ecumenism

18. The results of the dialogue which are being carried out both worldwide and regionally between churches have hardly been received on the local level.

> One continually hears that these dialogues and their results are "unknown" and "in general practically ignored". The dialogue results cannot be recognized and appropriated if they are not put forth. (FRG)
> Only theologians, ecumenical groups and individuals know the ecumenical dialogue. (Denmark)

19. This is certainly due to the lack of necessary information and the difficult hermeneutical task of making these dialogues accessible at the local level.

> It is repeatedly said: "We are not informed"; "We do not hear enough". The local clergy fail to implement theological courses with small groups. (FRG)

20. Nevertheless the essential reason for the evidently difficult — and up to now hardly successful — communication of the results of the interchurch dialogues on the local level lies deeper. It is clearly related to the fact that on the level of local ecumenical endeavours and on the level of the interchurch dialogues, the unity of the churches and of Christians — one and the same goal for all levels — is seen from different perspectives or in the light of different "interests", as has already been indicated, in view of the differing understandings of "doctrine" (cf. chapter IV/A and IV/B). In the area of the translocal dialogues the primary and main interest is the attainment of responsible agreement on questions of faith, doctrine, and church order in light of the apostolic witness of church tradition and the whole church; in the area of local ecumenism the primary and leading interest is lived community practised in mutuality and common service to one another. Correspondingly, that which should be overcome by means of ecumenical endeavours is, in the one area, the divergence of convictions, dissent and mutual criticism, and in the other area, the isolated coexistence of people or even antagonistic relations in daily church, social and personal life.

21. Of course this does not mean that there is a complete gap between the two areas. But it means that they cannot be related as directly and in such a clear-cut way as is so often attempted and so much desired.

22. As already said (cf. chapter IV/C), the questions dealt with in the interchurch dialogues are not unimportant, at least for the ecumenically interested and active groups, though they occasionally

say that they are. Rather, the traditional doctrinal questions, in their aspects and consequences related to praxis and lived community, are experienced as relevant for local ecumenical endeavours. And if the dialogue results are not heeded, that is because above all the praxis-related, life-determining, community-related dimensions are missed.

> The documents from ecumenical dialogues are expected to give practical suggestions (e.g. on handling problems such as divorce and remarriage). Therefore one sees them as irrelevant because, it is said, "our local praxis has already gone far beyond them." Doctrinal dialogues and their results are perceived "more in view of practical living together than theory". (FRG)
> The parishes are more interested in the possibilities of a common praxis of faith than in doctrinal agreement. (GDR)

23. Accordingly what "interests" them, e.g. in relation to the Lord's Supper, is not so much the question of the Real Presence or the eucharistic sacrifice but rather, as already mentioned, the way to deal with the elements left over, whether these are to be honoured or not, the frequency of celebration, communion under both kinds, and — above all — the possibility of a common celebration of the Lord's Supper (intercommunion).

24. With regard to the office of the ministry the interest is not with problems such as apostolic succession, or the sacramentality and non-repetition of ordination, but in the equivalence of the exercised office by the Catholic priest and the evangelical pastor (recognition of ministry) or the validity of a celebration of the Lord's Supper led by lay people.

25. In a similar way the interest with respect to confessionally mixed marriage is less in the question of the understanding of marriage (the sacramentality of marriage) than in such questions as "ecumenical weddings", mixed marriage legislation, eucharistic fellowship for the marriage partners, the complex problem of divorce/annulment/remarriage and of course the form of married life.

26. The same basic themes are definitely being debated on both levels, but under partly different aspects and therefore also in differing forms.

27. The first task for bringing about the necessary connection between doctrinal dialogues and local ecumenism is the recognition of the particularity of the interests and perspectives of each. From the local level it should be recognized that the concern for attaining a responsible theological agreement, with everything that includes, is indispensable for the genuineness and durability of the fellowship

which is sought. On the other hand, those included in the ecclesial-theological dialogues must be conscious that the interests at the local level are legitimately oriented to the concrete, lived fellowship and that traditional, controversial theological questions are experienced as really relevant only within these perspectives.

28. The second task would then be to bridge this "difference in interests" and to place both areas of ecumenical endeavour in closer relationship, so that the specifically local interests are more strongly taken into consideration in the themes and work of the doctrinal dialogues, and on the other hand the results of the doctrinal dialogues are "translated" into the specific fields of interest of the local congregations.

29. There are many examples of how such relating of both levels, with their specific fields of interests, can succeed. This appears to be the case in the Catholic/Lutheran document on the eucharist more than in other dialogue documents. It has been received with interest on the local level because it expressly contains aspects of lived eucharistic piety and discussion of the form of the celebration of the eucharist.

30. There is also the experience that where, on the basis of an attained theological consensus, the possibility of lived fellowship on the local level is opened up, oddly enough this possibility is hardly made use of.

> Almost ten years ago our Catholic bishop allowed eucharistic hospitality in special cases of mixed marriage. To begin with everyone was pleased and made use of this possibility. However it can be seen today that this new way is rarely mentioned or used. (France)

V. THE INFLUENCE
OF NON-DOCTRINAL FACTORS

1. It has long been well known that non-doctrinal factors play a big role in the unity and division of the churches and Christians. These factors contribute to the success or failure of ecumenical endeavours on the local level. Not only are questions of faith decisive at the local level. Ethnic or cultural identities, languages, social groups, ideologies, economic conditions, education, political position, personal relations and other factors like these influence ecumenical work on the local level. The fact that one may belong to a large (majority) church or to a small (minority) church is also one of the non-doctrinal factors, and this plays an important part in ecumenical relations. As church and social life are often closely interwoven, it is not easy to clearly recognize and evaluate these complex factors. In addition there are elements which are not specific to one area but still have an influence: e.g. the press or mass media play a decisive role in ecumenical life on the local level. Therefore the ecumenical ambivalence of these factors should be observed as they are able to promote or hinder Christian community.

A. The importance of the local context
2. Often the traditional confessional borders are identical with the borders which exist in general in social life between different groups of people and which arise out of reasons quite different from those of faith. A hardening of these barriers means added difficulty for cooperation between church parishes; a relaxing or effacement of these barriers is often the decisive element which makes ecumenical rapprochement possible. The general social and societal milieu in which Christian parishes try to live out their faith is therefore very significant.

> Clubs, associations, and parish councils have a reconciling and integrating role between parishes of different confessions. It is here that people of various confessions meet and make friends, are surprised by

the confessional separation... A club in a village brings people closer together than the churches are able to or generally intend. (Austria)

Local ecumenical endeavours appear to be quite significant to Asian communities even though the majority of those involved have little or no consciousness of being "ecumenical". The churches in many cases are able to draw upon the strong community consciousness and spirit which is characteristic of Asian community life. Celebrations of Christmas and community events, sports and singing competitions provide occasions to bring all Christians of local and even regional areas together sometimes for festivals lasting for days. Local ecumenical events and celebrations are also endorsed and supported by governmental concern for nation-building, especially in Indonesia and Singapore. (Indonesia)

That evangelical Christians are oriented towards the SPD and the Catholics to the CDU is very clear hear. This has been a very detrimental influence on ecumenism. (FRG)

3. The rise of new social identities provides a congenial milieu for the development of new ecumenical activities. Thus the motivation for unity seems to be more often present in new towns or settlements than in traditional situations. In these new settlements, the building up of the community is often connected with great, practically insurmountable difficulties. Especially in Europe and America, having this new identity is for many people who were previously involved in church life a sufficient motive to stay away now from the church. And yet such a new identity is also the trigger for ecumenical activity. In these new places, the ecumenical concern of Christians is part of their search for community. The awareness of being only a Christian minority in this place, as well as the often homogeneous sociological composition of the populations, strengthens this motivation.

In the new housing developments in which we all are "diaspora-congregations" no one is troubled by particular traditions and customs in our common work. (Netherlands)

4. Traditional social conditions often give rise to "ecumenical initiatives". Cooperative ecumenical work has existed under such conditions for a long time, and belongs to the life on the local level. Aspects of societal life also often have an ecumenical dimension here. It is part of the tradition that the local living Christian congregations share in local events. Strangely, it can be seen here that this initiative often does not come from the church communities or their active members. Those who organize village festivals or club parties hope for an ecumenical celebration and thus at a public social event joint representation of the church is requested. So on the basis of an "outside" initiative, individual ecumenical events arise, even in

places where no relationship exists between the Christian communities.

> The ecumenical harvest festival service on the last Sunday in September in the open with a harvest wagon procession, poetry by school children, blessing of vehicles, etc. . . .
> Ecumenically, that means that along with the exchange of ministers and the invitation and participation of members of both confessions, there are annual Bible weeks, a women's world day of prayer, services for inaugurations, flags, vehicles, houses, Christmas trees, roadside crosses and other consecrations, as has been hoped for by the organizers for years. (Austria)

5. Social and political problems are, in many local situations, the decisive factors for ecumenical initiatives (joint help for refugees, drug addicts, the sick and the aged). Confessional differences are considered secondary in the face of the necessity to unite in joint social or political service. Many an ecumenical group has thus developed from the recognition of a social need, and is carried further by this joint engagement.

> Factors which are ecumenically conciliating: joint aid actions, the sale of used paper, Christmas tree sales (for the benefit of the third world), organ renovations, church concerts, anniversary celebrations. Our "Guatemala coffee" is well-received ecumenically. (FRG)

6. However it must also be acknowledged here that, with a few exceptions, such an individual ecumenical response does not lead to the development of full ecclesial ecumenical community on the local level. The ecumenical approach present at this point can become a kind of "ecumenical alibi", which allows the local churches to continue to exist unchanged.

B. The influence of an environment of other religious faiths and ideologies

7. In Asia and Africa especially, but also in many parts of Europe and America, the behaviour and attitude of an environment which is predominantly other than Christian has a decisive influence on the ecumenical endeavours of the churches.

8. At first glance one would think that a difficult political situation or an anti-Christian stance on the part of the majority of a country's population would spur the church towards closer ecumenical cooperation. This is so in some situations.

> In some Indian states an anti-religion law was passed and the prejudices inherent in the caste system contributed to the joint Protestant, Catholic and Orthodox protest against this. (India)

9. However, difficulties and emergency situations in the economic or political area further the unity of the church much less than is usually supposed. The anti-church stance of a state or the majority of a society does not always act as the cement of unity. On the contrary it often leads to each community's withdrawing into itself and trying to survive on its own.

> Nevertheless it is not possible to speak of a unified front of the churches in a political context. The churches often prefer to tolerate silently and individually the injustices of governmental opposition. Two clear examples of injustice which the churches tolerate and try to solve by their own means, without working jointly together, are the refusal of the government to financially support Christian schools, as they do however for all public and other "private" schools, or the discrimination against Christians in questions of accommodation. (Israel)
> In any event, while it could be expected that the background would bring parishes and Christians closer together through necessity, this is actually hard to maintain. (FRG)

10. In most Asian and African countries the Christian population is not only a minority, but is also split into numerous denominations. Since in these countries national unity (nation-building) has a high political priority, efforts amongst Christians towards unity can have a socially positive and significant function. They can be assisted in these aims by the state as they help overcome the older divisions, tribal, local-national, linguistic, etc. However these very efforts towards unity among Christians often provoke resentment and opposition from the majority religion. Fear of such often militant reactions hinders the ecumenical efforts of the Christian churches.

C. The influence of personal elements

11. The discussion on the role of pastors and priests has already pointed to how great the influence of individuals can be in local ecumenism. This too is a kind of non-doctrinal factor which can further or hinder local ecumenism (cf. chapter II/B).

12. The ecumenical motivation or ideas of individual parish members are influenced and formed by such personal factors. For example, an event within the individual family, such as a mixed marriage, can lead to a radical change in the attitude towards other confessions. The confessional element can be used as an argument against a marriage with one of a "lower social class". If the marriage is however seen as a step upwards, then confessional arguments are quickly pushed aside as out-of-date and unimportant. The confessional argument is in the end made to serve or defend one's own

social situation and also perhaps the privileges connected with it. The arguments disappear when it is possible to come by a better social classification.

> Considered socially, the "new citizens" were "have-nots" had little prestige, so that it was thought worthless to trouble oneself with their religious views. The fact that the social viewpoint played a not unimportant role is to be seen in the small number of mixed marriages between native inhabitants and immigrants. This social reservation always shows itself in this last case, if the hindrances for marriage which are otherwise pushed forward fall away. (GDR)

13. This statement made on the basis of the example of mixed marriage is only an example of how quite personal, often self-seeking elements influence the ecumenical ideas of the individual. The fear of having to forfeit influence, name, financial privileges, etc. through ecumenical reconciliation, often leads to a personal, anti-ecumenical attitude. The hope of acquiring all these can result in remarkable ecumenical openness.

14. On the local level strongly established churches are often particularly faced with such questions. The struggle for unity brings hesitation and fear with it, not so much in relation to exclusively theological questions, but in relation to church property, personal ambition, positions of authority within the church, the denominational instinct of self-preservation, financial advantages and privileges, etc.

> It must be admitted that such an ecumenical goal fails due to the hostility of a few privileged, who will oppose every progress within this area for the sake of a misunderstood confessional identity. (France)
> Church leaders pray for unity, but in reality they fear it. (Indonesia)
> It may not be completely wrong to say that the number one problem for the malaise in the ecumenical movement is strong hierarchical structures... (M)any, if not all, good resolutions and recommendations... get stuck at the hierarchical level... Another sad fact that should be mentioned here is that some of the western churches (supporting mission boards) support such conservative groups and help them financially to create splinter churches. This is at least true in India. I only wish that they would try to understand the meaning of the priesthood of all believers. (India)

D. The ecumenical ambivalence of "non-doctrinal" factors

15. "Non-doctrinal" factors are for the most part ambivalent in their ecumenical significance. The same fact can be either a help or a hindrance on the path towards unity, depending on the area or situation. Thus nearly all of these factors can be judged at the same time both as negative and positive. It can on the one hand be associated

with the idea of "sin", insofar as self-interest, self-seeking, self-assertion, envy or laziness are involved. On the other hand it can be a catalyst, a trigger for a deep-reaching ecumenical renewal, even though efforts for unity should in no way be based solely on such factors. As these factors do not remain static but are in a dynamic process of development, their importance can change within a relatively short time.

16. The ambivalence of "non-doctrinal" factors calls for closer study and consideration not only on the local level but also in inter-church dialogues. Of course this is a difficult task, as these factors are closely linked, and specific, in their variety and particularity, to the local area and cannot therefore serve as the object of a translocal dialogue. It would however be important for the local parish to recognize and evaluate these factors and their influence. The theological questions behind all this must be dealt with, and this calls for additional work.

17. The first need would be for a close consideration of that which constitutes the church on the local level. Non-doctrinal factors often play a considerable role in that they either further or hinder community. There is probably no place where this is not the case. How far can and may a local parish be built up on such factors, and thereby be dependent on them? When do they endanger church existence on the local level? This question needs closer discussion in ecumenical dialogues.

18. A second and closely connected question would be that of the relationship between faith and life in society. This connection is vital for every church and every parish. To take God as Creator means that faith cannot be confined only to the "spiritual" realm, like faith convictions, doctrine and piety; it demands a consideration also of non-doctrinal factors which affect human society. To take God as Redeemer means acknowledging the incarnation, and thereby taking seriously the world and humanity in all their dimensions. However Good Friday and Easter do not allow any absolutizing of "non-doctrinal" factors. Their destructive aspects are overcome in faith in Jesus Christ and in fellowship with him (Gal. 3:28). Finally the Holy Spirit is the certainty for the church that its unity, holiness and universality depend in the last analysis on the presence of God alone.

19. The questions raised by non-doctrinal factors are in no way specifically ecumenical questions related only to ecclesial unity. In this, as in many other points, our study shows that in ecumenical endeavours on the local level, one finally comes across the questions which are essential for the life of every Christian church and con-

gregation, whether or not it is concerned with ecumenical relations. Thus the specifically ecumenical questions of the local congregation are bound to the total Christian and ecclesial life with its questions and joys, its need and its promise.